# The Making of a First Lady

'We want our children . . . to know that the only limit to the height of your achievements is the reach of your dreams and your willingness to work for them.'

Born and raised in a working-class neighbourhood in Chicago, how did Michelle Obama rise to become a top graduate, a powerful lawyer and a global icon as wife to the President of the USA?

Find out in this empowering life story.

**Also available by Dawne Allette,
and published by Tamarind Books:**

BARACK OBAMA: THE MAKING OF A PRESIDENT

**Other biographies from Tamarind Books
(for younger readers):**

MALORIE BLACKMAN – Author
BENJAMIN ZEPHANIAH – Poet
RUDOLPH WALKER – Actor
DAVID GRANT – Vocal Coach
CHINWE ROY – Artist
JIM BRATHWAITE – Entrepreneur
BARONESS SCOTLAND – QC and Politician
SAMANTHA TROSS – Surgeon
LORD JOHN TAYLOR – Barrister
THE LIFE OF STEPHEN LAWRENCE

**Tamarind Books** publish multicultural
children's books for a multicultural world.
We believe that all children should be valued for
who they are and should live in an environment
which respects their own identity, culture and
heritage; and they should meet people like
themselves in the books they read.

**For a full list of other Tamarind Books titles see:**
www.**tamarindbooks**.co.uk

# MICHELLE OBAMA

## The Making of a First Lady

## by Dawne Allette

Tamarind

MICHELLE OBAMA: THE MAKING OF A FIRST LADY
A TAMARIND BOOK 978 1 848 53029 4

First published in Great Britain by Tamarind Books,
a division of Random House Children's Books
A Random House Group Company

Tamarind Books edition published 2010

1 3 5 7 9 10 8 6 4 2

The Random House Group Limited supports the Forest Stewardship Council (FSC),
the leading international forest certification organization. All our titles that are
printed on Greenpeace-approved FSC-certified paper carry the FSC logo. Our paper
procurement policy can be found at www.rbooks.co.uk/environment.

Set in Humanist 12.5/18.75pt

Tamarind Books are published by Random House Children's Books,
61–63 Uxbridge Road, London W5 5SA

www.**tamarindbooks**.co.uk
www.**kidsatrandomhouse**.co.uk
www.**rbooks**.co.uk

Addresses for companies within The Random House Group Limited can be found
at: www.randomhouse.co.uk/offices.htm

THE RANDOM HOUSE GROUP Limited Reg. No. 954009

A CIP catalogue record for this book is available from the British Library.

Printed and bound in Great Britain by
CPI Bookmarque, Croydon, CR0 4TD

*For Christine, Doreen,*
*Verna and Margaret*

*four phenomenal women*

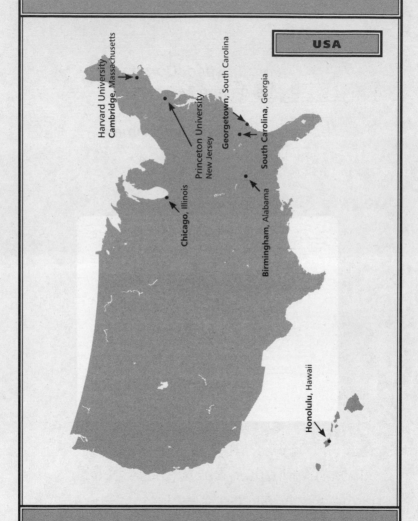

**Michelle Obama** grew up in Chicago, but studied elsewhere in the USA, and married a man who grew up mostly in Hawaii. These places are marked on this map, along with the birthplaces of some of her ancestors.

USA

Harvard University
Cambridge, Massachusetts

Princeton University
New Jersey

Georgetown, South Carolina

South Carolina, Georgia

Birmingham, Alabama

Chicago, Illinois

Honolulu, Hawaii

*'We're all linked through our histories of growth and survival in this country'*

Michelle Obama

# PROLOGUE

*'Nothing in my life ever would have predicted that I would be standing here . . .'*

The girls at Elizabeth Garrett Anderson Language College in Islington, North London were told to prepare for 'a very special guest'. No one knew who the guest was. They took turns guessing who it might be, but it was not until she stood on the stage that it became clear who it was. They were stunned.

It was April 2009, and Michelle Obama, wife of the newly elected President of the United States, Barack Obama, was making her first official trip to Great Britain as America's First

Lady. On day one, she toured the cancer ward at a London hospital with Sarah Brown, the wife of Britain's Prime Minister, Gordon Brown. She spoke with several patients and everyone responded warmly. Later, a visit with her husband to Buckingham Palace to meet the Queen made headlines in all the major newspapers. Her Majesty broke with tradition by resting her hand momentarily across Michelle's back just after she greeted her. Michelle did the same in return. This was totally against normal royal protocol – the Queen did not touch her visitors other than to shake hands. A photographer captured the moment and the pictures went around the world.

Now, on her second day, Michelle chose to visit a school. This was significant as Michelle is very interested in education. While campaigning with her husband as he ran for President of the United States, a ten-year-old African American girl told Michelle that if Obama won the election, it would 'be historical'. Michelle asked the girl what that might mean to her. In tears, the girl answered that it would mean that she would be able to imagine anything for herself too.

Education, Michelle now told the girls at Elizabeth Garrett Anderson School, was the main reason she was standing here before them. Education could change lives, and a good education was something every girl in the school could use to change *their* lives for the better. Working hard at school was the first step towards being able to choose good careers for themselves. She did not understand why some people thought it wasn't 'cool' to do your best and try to learn. When she was their age, she told them, she hadn't ever played truant from school, missed lessons or turned up late. For her, being educated and informed had always been important. It would open doors for them so that they too could be leaders in whatever they chose to do.

The girls gave Michelle their full attention. Teachers told them this kind of thing all the time – as did their parents – but to hear it from Michelle Obama, who told them how she had been brought up with little money or social standing yet was now the First Lady of the USA, was different. It was inspiring.

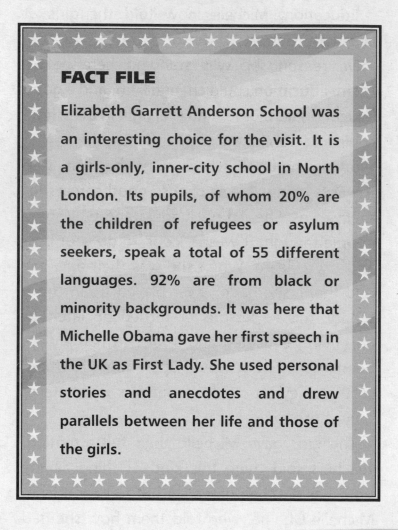

**FACT FILE**

Elizabeth Garrett Anderson School was an interesting choice for the visit. It is a girls-only, inner-city school in North London. Its pupils, of whom 20% are the children of refugees or asylum seekers, speak a total of 55 different languages. 92% are from black or minority backgrounds. It was here that Michelle Obama gave her first speech in the UK as First Lady. She used personal stories and anecdotes and drew parallels between her life and those of the girls.

Michelle Obama comes from a working-class background.

She overcame racial prejudice and low expectations to earn degrees from Princeton University and Harvard Law School, two of America's top educational institutions.

She walked away from a lucrative law career to work in public service.

Michelle is raising two daughters and has played a tremendous role in her husband's political career.

Here is her amazing story.

# CHAPTER ONE

*'Deep down inside, I'm still that little girl who grew up on the South Side of Chicago.'*

Michelle LaVaughn Robinson was born in Chicago on 17 January 1964. Her father, Fraser Robinson III, was a labourer for the city of Chicago's water department. He swept floors, cleaned up litter and scrubbed the walkways of a water filtration plant. Her mother, Marian, had worked as a secretary before she married Fraser. After her first child – a boy, Craig – was born, Marian decided to stay at home and be a full-time mother. Michelle was born 22 months after Craig.

## FACT FILE

Chicago is in the state of Illinois, in the heart of the American Midwest. By 1964, when Michelle was born, Chicago had a large black population. Before then, further south, harsh laws had segregated the black and white population and prevented blacks from voting in elections. This led many African Americans to move to northern cities. Factory work was widely available, but the number of jobs was declining and white families were moving away to the suburbs. For the black community, opportunities for good housing and education were very limited.

The Robinsons lived in an apartment on a busy main road called South Park. It was in the heart of Chicago's 'Black Belt', a district of crowded, substandard flats where African Americans had lived for decades.

When Michelle was two years old, the American civil rights leader, Dr Martin Luther King Jr, moved to Chicago.

He wanted to bring attention to the fact that black residents there were treated like second-class citizens, kept in the city's 'ghetto' by estate agents who discriminated against them. Others joined him to campaign for better jobs, better schools and better housing.

Dr King was shocked that white crowds responded to demands by African Americans for equal rights with so many threats and with violence. During one demonstration in the city, he was hit in the head by a brick but he continued to lead the march in the face of great personal danger.

In these turbulent times, Craig and Michelle were protected by their parents. The Robinsons were determined not to let prejudice cripple their children's self-esteem or stop them from working towards a successful future. Michelle clearly remembers her father telling her she was as good as anyone else. Life, he told her, was about discipline and about setting goals – it was not, and should not be, about skin colour.

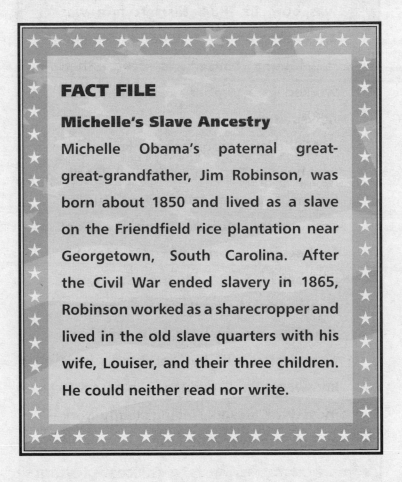

## FACT FILE

### Michelle's Slave Ancestry

Michelle Obama's paternal great-great-grandfather, Jim Robinson, was born about 1850 and lived as a slave on the Friendfield rice plantation near Georgetown, South Carolina. After the Civil War ended slavery in 1865, Robinson worked as a sharecropper and lived in the old slave quarters with his wife, Louiser, and their three children. He could neither read nor write.

Jim's second son and Michelle's great-grandfather, Fraser Robinson, was born in 1884. His left arm was amputated after a childhood accident. He taught himself to read, then worked in a lumber factory and sold newspapers.

Michelle's grandfather, Fraser Jr, was born in 1912 to Fraser and Rosella Robinson. He was an excellent student and orator before leaving school to become a bricklayer. He lost his job around 1932 during the Great Depression. The local economy was in a shambles and the legal rights of blacks were restricted by anti-black laws known as 'Jim Crow' laws. So Fraser Jr moved to Chicago. Finding steady work in Chicago was not easy because of racial discrimination. He eventually got a job at the post office.

Michelle's father, Fraser III, was born in Chicago in 1935, the son of Fraser Jr and LaVaughn Robinson. He grew up in a South Side housing project roughly akin to a large council estate in the UK.

Michelle's mother, Marian Shields, was also descended from slaves, according to recently uncovered material published in *The New York Times*. The family's earliest known ancestor was Melvinia 'Mattie' Shields McGruder, born a slave about 1844 in South Carolina. After her master died in 1850, Mattie was bequeathed to heirs and taken to the state of Georgia.

While still a teenager, Mattie was impregnated by an unknown white man and gave birth to Dolphus T. Shields. Dolphus moved to Birmingham, Alabama, where he ran a carpentry business and co-founded the Trinity Baptist Church.

Michelle's great-grandfather, Robert Lee Shields, was a railroad porter. His son, Purnell Shields, moved to Chicago around 1930 and worked as a house painter and factory worker.

Marian Shields, Michelle's mother, was born in 1937, one of seven children of Purnell Shields and Rebecca Jumper, a nurse.

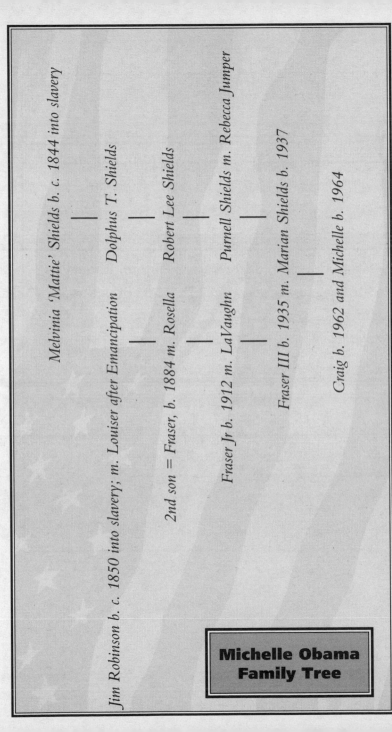

Melvinia 'Mattie' Shields b. c. 1844 into slavery

Dolphus T. Shields

Robert Lee Shields

Purnell Shields m. Rebecca Jumper

Fraser III b. 1935 m. Marian Shields b. 1937

Jim Robinson b. c. 1850 into slavery; m. Louiser after Emancipation

2nd son = Fraser, b. 1884 m. Rosella

Fraser Jr b. 1912 m. LaVaughn

Craig b. 1962 and Michelle b. 1964

**Michelle Obama Family Tree**

# CHAPTER TWO

*'I am an example of what is possible when girls, from the very beginning of their lives, are loved and nurtured by the people around them.'*

When Michelle was six years old, her father moved the family to a better neighbourhood on the South Side. The family rented the top floor of a small house that belonged to Michelle's aunt. Michelle shared a room with her brother. A divider turned the dining room into two bedrooms for the children. A childhood friend described Michelle's bedroom as being about the size of a large closet – smaller than any room she had ever seen before.

Michelle liked to play with her dolls and Easy-Bake Oven set. She owned a black Barbie doll, a Ken doll and a dolls' house. With the toy oven, she could bake simple recipes (a light bulb in the stove provided the heat source). All of this was somehow stuffed into her tiny bedroom.

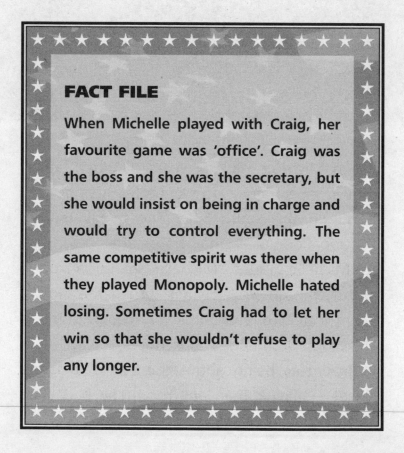

**FACT FILE**

When Michelle played with Craig, her favourite game was 'office'. Craig was the boss and she was the secretary, but she would insist on being in charge and would try to control everything. The same competitive spirit was there when they played Monopoly. Michelle hated losing. Sometimes Craig had to let her win so that she wouldn't refuse to play any longer.

Michelle's aunt was a piano teacher. She gave lessons to Michelle. No one had to encourage young Michelle to practise. She did so for hours on end. Sometimes her mother had to ask her to stop and rest. But her piano skills were to prove helpful to Craig. He confessed later that, when he was on his high school basketball team and feeling nervous the night before a big game, Michelle would play the piano to help him relax.

At weekends, both children carried out chores. Michelle was in charge of the bathroom and toilet. She had to mop the floor and scrub the sink. She also shared the washing up of dishes with her brother. Michelle would do the washing up on Tuesdays, Thursdays and Saturdays, and it was Craig's turn on Mondays, Wednesdays and Fridays. Sunday was up for grabs! Michelle's mother did not have to pester her to do her chores. Marian later told a newspaper interviewer that she felt as though Michelle raised herself from about nine years old. She believed her daughter had her head on straight very early in life.

Michelle's father was a strong influence in her life. Although he had not been to university, Fraser read widely and was an intelligent man.

He expected good behaviour from his children, and if Michelle or Craig behaved badly he would discipline them without having to raise his voice. He often expressed his disappointment with an icy stare. Michelle later recalled how she had never wanted to disappoint him.

Michelle's paternal grandparents, Fraser Jr and his wife LaVaughn, lived nearby. On most Sundays and national holidays – such as Thanksgiving and Christmas – the family visited them.

Grandfather Fraser was an avid fan of music, especially Chicago-style blues and jazz. He entertained them all with his favourite records and the family spent many hours together while Michelle's father and grandfather recalled family stories and traded jokes.

## FACT FILE

Chicago is the home of the 'blues'. When African Americans migrated to the city from the south, they brought along plantation chants and church gospel music, which then became mixed up with urban jazz. Music flourished in South Side 'juke joints' where Muddy Waters, Howlin' Wolf and other bluesmen crafted simple, powerful songs. This style of music was a huge influence on British groups in the early 1960s, like The Beatles and The Rolling Stones, who successfully recorded some of the same songs themselves.

At home, Marian, Michelle's mother, cooked fresh meals for the family every night. Macaroni-and-cheese casserole was a family favourite, along with fried chicken made with Marian's special ingredient: Ritz crackers crumbled in the batter. Michelle has since admitted that she did not inherit her mother's talent for cooking!

Adding to the flavour of the meals were lively debates about current events. At the dinner table there were always discussions about different issues. Michelle liked to take part in these discussions and express her opinion.

Perhaps her parents had these dinner discussions in mind when they took out a small advert in the Harvard Law School yearbook in 1988, the year Michelle graduated from law school. Leaving a message for graduating children was a tradition at the school, and the message Fraser and Marian came up with possessed their trademark humour:

> *'We knew you would
> do this fifteen years ago
> when we could never
> make you shut up.'*

# CHAPTER THREE

*'My dad was our rock.'*

When Michelle's father Fraser was in his early 30s, he was diagnosed with multiple sclerosis. MS is a disease that affects the ability of the brain and spinal cord to communicate with each other. The disease causes loss of muscular coordination and problems with speaking and swallowing. Its cause is unknown and there is no known cure.

Despite his illness, Fraser volunteered to help the Democratic Party campaign in his neighbourhood. This meant a great deal of travelling around the community – knocking on doors and trying to convince people to register and vote. If people weren't registered, then they couldn't vote when elections came round. Many people in the community supported the Democratic Party, and Fraser wanted all their supporters to be registered and prepared to vote in the next elections.

**FACT FILE**

There are two main political parties in America. The Republican Party has social and economic principles similar to Britain's Conservative Party, while the Democratic Party is closer to the Labour Party. Michelle's family supported the Democrats. Barack Obama would later run for office as a Democrat.

As her father's illness became worse, Michelle spent many Saturdays supporting him. She held his hand as he walked slowly from door to door and struggled to climb the steps of houses. Michelle said her introduction to politics was sitting in her neighbours' kitchens, listening to their opinions, concerns and the dreams they had for their children.

The Robinsons' dream was that someday Michelle and Craig would enjoy some of the material things that they could not provide for them. They believed that a good education was the key to success and economic advancement – the same message Michelle gave when she spoke at the school in England more than thirty years later.

From an early age, Michelle learned how to study well. She skipped second grade just like her brother had done. Since she was only allowed to watch one hour of television a night, she developed a love for reading. As she got older, she composed short stories, writing intently in a spiral notebook.

One of the problems facing young black

people on the South Side was the deplorable state of the schools. Many schools lacked books and adequate supplies, even pencils and desks.

through to Senior) correspond to UK Years 10-13.

From sixth grade (Year 7) upwards, the curriculum includes both compulsory subjects such as maths, English and science, where students may be divided into groups for differing levels of achievement, and elective classes such as foreign languages or art.

There is no national curriculum like in the UK. Instead, each state determines which courses must be followed in order to graduate from high school. In practice, the coursework is very similar in all parts of the US and on completion, at the end of the twelfth grade (at age 18), students receive their high school diplomas. Without a high school diploma, career opportunities can be

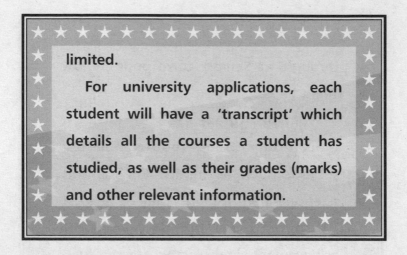

In the sixth grade at Bryn Mawr School, Michelle got a fortunate break. After years of lobbying by residents, the school she attended received a government grant to start a gifted-students programme. As one of the brightest children in the school, Michelle qualified for the programme.

This allowed her to start studying French three years before most students were offered the subject. She thrived in this setting, not only from the intellectual stimulation, but also from a growing sense of personal pride and accomplishment.

She left the school at the top of her class.

The next decision facing the Robinson family was choosing which high school Michelle should attend. Craig was going to a Catholic high school. (In America, as in the UK, children do not have to be Catholic to attend a Catholic school.) Michelle picked Whitney M. Young Magnet School, a high school for students who planned to attend college after graduation.

It took a lot of guts for a thirteen year old to travel ten miles in each direction to the new school on her own. She made the long trip back and forth by bus and train, spending up to three hours a day in transit. But she never complained, not even when snow covered the city with a thick white blanket.

Michelle made many friends at her new school. They were from different races and some were richer than others, but they all had one thing in common – the desire to learn. Fellow students not only noticed her energy, but also her budding sense of fashion. With babysitting money, she purchased one of the classiest handbags she could find and joyfully strutted down the hallways of Whitney Young.

A neighbour commented that young Michelle was elegant and could have been a model. Even then, Michelle thought carefully about what she wore, although she never would have dreamed that her personal style would be copied by so many women today.

**FACT FILE**

Michelle appeared on the cover of fashion magazine *Vogue* in Spring 2009, confirming her as a style icon.

During her four years of high school, Michelle took advanced placement courses. These allow high school students to study more advanced, college-level courses. She did well academically. She was also treasurer for the student council and participated in many extracurricular activities. One of her classmates later told a newspaper reporter that Michelle hadn't 'goofed off' like many of the other students.

Even then, she had given the impression of being on a very focused path. (This was in contrast to her future husband, Barack Obama, who described himself as a 'sort of goof-off' in high school.)

**FACT FILE**

Michelle's favourite musician when she was a teenager was Stevie Wonder.

Although she excelled in her classes, Michelle did not naturally do well on standardized tests. Several of her teachers told her that her test scores weren't good enough to get her admitted to an 'Ivy League', or top-ranked, college. In a campaign speech in 2008, Michelle explained: 'If my future were determined just by my performance on a standardized test, I wouldn't be here. I guarantee you that.'

Her brother, Craig, had been accepted at Princeton University, one of the oldest Ivy

League schools. Michelle visited him on campus and saw that he was doing well. She decided that she was determined to attend the same university, even though her careers counsellor discouraged her from doing so.

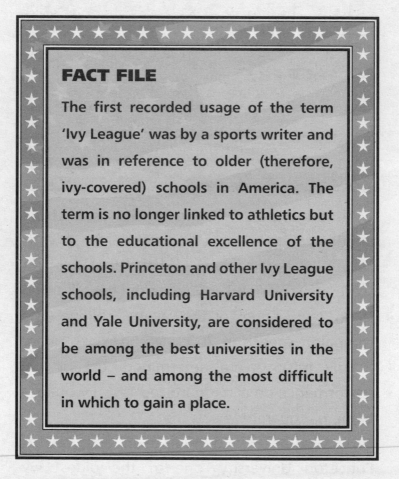

**FACT FILE**

The first recorded usage of the term 'Ivy League' was by a sports writer and was in reference to older (therefore, ivy-covered) schools in America. The term is no longer linked to athletics but to the educational excellence of the schools. Princeton and other Ivy League schools, including Harvard University and Yale University, are considered to be among the best universities in the world – and among the most difficult in which to gain a place.

Michelle didn't listen – and went ahead with her application. When she finally got her acceptance letter from Princeton, she was ecstatic. Her hard work and persistence had paid off.

In the autumn of 1981, seventeen-year-old Michelle Robinson kissed her parents goodbye and headed for Princeton, New Jersey. As it turned out, the Princeton admissions board had looked at more than Michelle's standard test scores. They had also factored in her overall performance at Whitney Young and recognized, from the example of her brother, that the Robinson kids were prepared to work hard to get good results.

# CHAPTER FOUR

*'I remember being shocked by college students who drove BMWs. I didn't even know parents who drove BMWs.'*

Coming from a poor, inner-city community, entering Princeton University meant an enormous adjustment for Michelle. Everything about the place radiated privilege – privilege that had been off-limits to black students for most of the institution's long history.

The school's legacy of exclusion was summed up in the early 1900s by Woodrow Wilson, president of Princeton before he became the 28th president of the United States. He wrote that 'no negro has ever applied for admission, and it seems extremely unlikely that the question [of black enrolment] will ever assume a practical form.' When an African American student did apply in 1936 and was accepted, he was refused enrolment when he showed up on campus.

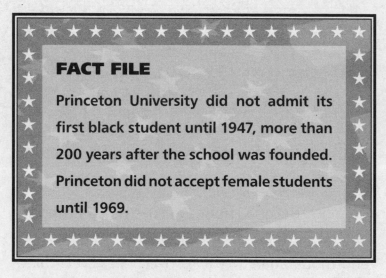

**FACT FILE**

Princeton University did not admit its first black student until 1947, more than 200 years after the school was founded. Princeton did not accept female students until 1969.

There were few blacks in Michelle's freshman class when she arrived on campus in 1981 – only 94 out of more than 1,100 students. For the first time in her life, she experienced what it was really like to be a minority.

Her mother later said that because Michelle hadn't talked about it a lot she assumed that her daughter had not let the issue of race bother

her. But Michelle couldn't help but be bothered. The white mother of Michelle's first room-mate complained when she found out that her daughter would be sharing a room with a black student. She demanded that her daughter be placed immediately with another white student since she wasn't used to living with black people.

There were other incidents that made Michelle and others within the African American student body feel unwelcome. Newspaper articles were sometimes slipped under the doors of black students. These articles argued that their presence on campus brought down academic standards. What made these innuendoes upsetting to hardworking students like Michelle was that the number of blacks was far fewer than the number of 'legacy' students. These were students who had been admitted to Princeton not because of their superior grades, but because their parents were alumni, or graduates, of the school.

Michelle's best friend, Suzanne Alele, a Nigerian-born computer wiz, often talked about the racial divide on campus – how white students they knew from class would pass them on the campus grounds and pretend not to see them. Michelle, however, mixed well with students from other races, recognizing that the percentage of students that did not appreciate students of colour was not representative of the majority of students.

To support herself financially, she did babysitting, gave piano lessons and even learned how to train dogs. Like many students both in the US and in the UK, she also had to take out large student loans to help pay for her tuition.

Craig's presence on campus during her first two years at Princeton was a big help to Michelle. Craig not only did well in the classroom, but was the Ivy League Player of the Year at Princeton during her freshman and sophomore years. Being the sister of a basketball star gave her a certain social prestige, but even more importantly, having Craig nearby to talk to was reassuring.

Having an outspoken sister on campus,

## FACT FILE

### VOLUNTEER WORK

Even though volunteering was a luxury she could scarcely afford, Michelle found time to take a job at an after-school programme for the children of Princeton's maintenance and lunchroom staff. It turned out to be one of her most satisfying experiences in college. The centre's director recognized that Michelle had a natural ability to bond with children. One of them was the director's own son, Jonathan Brasuell, who later told a newspaper that Michelle would delight him by playing 'Linus and Lucy', a famous jazz piano piece from the *Peanuts* television specials. He said he could not go a week without hearing Michelle play it for him – and Michelle always did.

however, had its trying moments for Craig. One day he called his mother and complained that Michelle was telling the university professors that they were teaching French incorrectly. Michelle believed that her professor should be teaching more conversational French rather than focusing on literary French. By then, Marian knew better than to interfere with her strong-willed daughter. She told Craig just to pretend that he didn't know his sister!

Michelle studied sociology at Princeton. Her senior-year essay was entitled 'Princeton-Educated Blacks and the Black Community'. She conducted a survey with African American alumni about whether they felt more comfortable or less comfortable with whites and blacks before, during, and after attending the school.

In the essay Michelle examined her own feelings about race. She wrote:

*'My experiences at Princeton have made me far more aware of my "blackness" than ever before.'* She continued that: *'No matter how liberal and open-minded some of my white*

*professors and classmates try to be toward me, I sometimes feel like a visitor on campus, as if I really don't belong. Regardless of the circumstances under which I interact with whites at Princeton, it often seems as if, to them, I will always be black first and a student second.'*

By this time, Michelle had developed an interest in law. She reflected on this ambition in her senior paper, writing, somewhat humorously:

*'I find myself striving for many of the same goals as my white classmates – acceptance to a prestigious graduate or professional school.'*

About to graduate *cum laude* (with honours) from Princeton in 1985, she set her sights on the best law school in America: Harvard. Once again, a counsellor told her that she might not be accepted. Once again, she turned a deaf ear to this and applied anyway.

She made it.

In September 1985, at the age of 21, Michelle arrived on the campus of Harvard Law School ready to begin the next stage of her academic journey.

**Above:** A little girl from the South Side, with her father Fraser, mother Marian and brother Craig

Michelle as a proud graduate

A couple in love

Michelle and Barack – with their mothers – on their wedding day

The growing family

Reaching out to voters on the campaign trail

Inauguration Day – and Michelle becomes America's First Lady

Michelle inspires students at a London school

The First Lady at work

The Queen breaks with royal protocol to greet Michelle

Stepping out in style

Life in the White House

# CHAPTER FIVE

*'By the time she got to Harvard, she had answered the question. She could be both brilliant and black.'*

The qualms and conflicts that Michelle had experienced at Princeton gave way to a new sense of confidence at Harvard. Her intelligence so impressed classmate Verna Williams that she specifically asked Michelle to be her partner on a mock-trial case. Williams said that Michelle was very smart, charismatic and well-spoken.

Michelle made an equally strong impression on her law school professors. Harvard is famous for the way students compete ruthlessly for top grades and vie for their professors' attention. Michelle got noticed for her thoughtful responses to thorny questions posed by her professors. Charles J. Ogletree, Michelle's academic advisor there, believed that she had wrestled with questions about her background and had worked out that she could retain her identity as an African American while pursuing her goals at an elite university.

Her senior essay at Princeton had been part of the process of defining herself. She wrote in that paper that her experiences *made my goals to actively utilize my resources to benefit the black community more desirable.'*

As she had done at Princeton, Michelle got involved in African American organizations at Harvard. She helped arrange meetings between students and Harvard alumni that gave students career tips and 'networking' opportunities as they began to search for jobs 'in the real world'.

With the date of her own graduation approaching in May 1988, she had to think seriously about her own career. Where would she go? What would she do? Apart from her own ambitions, she knew she needed to make some money as she had large student loans to repay.

---

**FACT FILE**

**'GIVING BACK'**

At Harvard, Michelle's goal of 'giving back' to the community took the form of working at a legal aid office run by the students. She committed herself to 20 hours a week to help poor clients who couldn't afford a lawyer. Ronald Tolbert, a classmate who worked with Michelle at the aid bureau, said she handled some of the more difficult cases and his reported opinion was that she really seemed to *care* about the people she worked with.

---

She finally applied for and got a job in Chicago at the law firm of Sidley & Austin. Here she was to specialize in cases involving marketing and advertising.

In the summer of 1989, Michelle was given a routine assignment at the law firm. She was asked to supervise a first-year law student with the unusual name of Barack Hussein Obama.

This assignment was to change her life.

## FACT FILE

### BARNEY THE DINOSAUR

During Michelle's first job at Sidley & Austin, she handled the account for Barney the dinosaur. Barney was a purple Tyrannosaurus rex character who starred in a television show produced for pre-school children and was the creation of a former school teacher whose son loved dinosaurs. Barney became Michelle's 'client'. She helped to manage the trademark protection and distribution of Barney merchandise and later negotiated with public television stations that wanted to broadcast the show.

# CHAPTER SIX

## 'Barack Obama was the real deal.'

Before she met Barack Obama, Michelle had heard other lawyers talking about him. They said he was one of the most brilliant first-year students ever to attend Harvard Law School. Secretaries who had caught sight of him during his job interview gossiped about how charming and good looking he was.

Michelle had her doubts. She thought he might be 'a little nerdy' or like some of the law students she had met at Harvard, could be puffed up with a giant ego. 'Here's this good-looking, smooth-talking guy,' she later told a Chicago reporter. 'I've been down this road before.'

Michelle had, of course, had a number of boyfriends, but no one very serious. According to her brother Craig, she had impossibly high standards when it came to men. She had even told her mother that her career plans did not include getting distracted by romance.

When they met, Barack found Michelle immediately appealing. She was tall and statuesque, he later wrote, with a good sense of humour and what he called a 'touching' sense of vulnerability behind her energetic personality.

As his mentor, Michelle saw Barack every day. She found that he was not only as smart as her colleagues had said, but he was easy to talk to. He told her about growing up in Hawaii, the son of a black African father and a white American mother.

Barack was six feet, two inches tall, while Michelle was five feet, eleven inches in bare feet. She liked the fact that he was tall, just like her father and brother, so she didn't have to look down at him. She told her girlfriends that she couldn't help but notice that he was quite handsome, although she wasn't keen on his fashion sense (a very 'bad' sports jacket), nor on his smoking habit.

Their first date happened unexpectedly. Barack offered to drive Michelle home after a company picnic. Along the way they spotted a Baskin-Robbins ice cream parlour, and he offered to buy her a cone. As they sat on the kerb eating ice cream, Barack told Michelle about working at Baskin-Robbins when he was a teenager and how hard it was to look cool in a brown apron and cap.

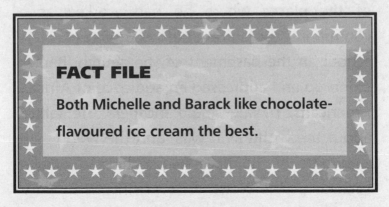

**FACT FILE**

Both Michelle and Barack like chocolate-flavoured ice cream the best.

She told him that when she was a girl, she had refused to eat anything except peanut butter and jelly sandwiches. When they finished their ice cream cones, Barack asked Michelle if he could kiss her!

For their first *real* date Michelle and Barack went to see the movie *Do the Right Thing*, directed by Spike Lee. Years later, Barack met Lee and thanked him profusely. He then explained to the puzzled director that it was while watching *Do the Right Thing* that Michelle let him touch her knee for the first time.

One day Barack invited Michelle to a meeting at a church on Chicago's South Side. It was one of the places where he had worked as a community organizer before going to law school. In the basement of the church, Barack stood up and addressed an audience of African Americans, mostly single mothers. He talked about the world as it was, and the world as it should be. All too often, he pointed out, people settled for the world as it was, even when it didn't reflect their values and aspirations.

Michelle was impressed. She saw a person who not only shared her commitment to social justice, but who could also navigate between the privileged white world of Sidley & Austin and the struggling African American world of the South Side. A man who could shed his jacket and tie and talk powerfully and convincingly to 'folks who were like me, who grew up like me, who were challenged and struggling in ways that I never would.'

'I knew then and there,' she later told audiences during the 2008 US presidential campaign, 'that Barack Obama was the real deal.'

But one thing that did *not* impress her was Barack's car. Michelle later said: 'His first car had so much rust that there was a rusted hole in the passenger door. You could see the ground when you were driving by. He loved that car. It would shake ferociously when it would start up. I thought, *'This brother is not interested in ever making a dime'*. I would just have to love him for his values.'

The couple became inseparable. Michelle took Barack home to meet her parents and brother. The comparison to Barack's own family was stark. His father had left when Barack was only two years old, and his mother had lived abroad in Indonesia for much of his childhood. He had been brought up mostly by his grandparents in Hawaii. The two-parent Robinson family stirred in him a longing for stability and a sense of belonging.

Marian saw Barack as a polite and interesting young man. She later told a reporter that he hadn't talked about himself or his achievements. He hadn't even told them that he was running for president of the *Harvard Law Review*. This was the university's highly acclaimed law journal and Barack made national news when he went on to become its president. It was the first time in the *Law Review*'s 104-year history that a black man had been elected president or editor.

Michelle was still very close to her brother Craig. He had always been a strong role model for her – setting a level of academic achievement she worked hard to match – and she valued his opinion. Craig had played two seasons with the Manchester (UK) Giants before becoming an investment banker. He had met all types of people as an athlete, many of whom were competitive men. Michelle asked Craig to spend time with her new boyfriend and come back to her with his opinion.

Craig considered where and how he could accomplish this task. He settled on the basketball court. He and his father believed that you could tell what somebody was really like by playing basketball with them. Fortunately for the purposes of Craig's 'test', Barack loved basketball. He had played on his high school team in Hawaii and was confident enough to agree to get on court with the six-foot-six former basketball star.

After the game was over, Craig reported back to his sister that Barack's ball-playing was like his personality – intense but level-headed. He said that Barack was not afraid to shoot the ball when he was open, but he was not a ball hog, either. He was a fair player, too, in that he didn't just pass the ball to Craig because he was Michelle's brother.

Michelle called a friend from Harvard Law School to tell her the good news – she had this great new guy in her life: Barack Obama. As Michelle told her more, the friend realized that Michelle had fallen in love.

According to one journalist's opinion, Michelle was attracted to Barack's diverse background and to the fact that he was different from the many smooth-talking men she had met. He had the same moral character and sense of social justice that she valued and loved in her father.

The couple spent a great deal of time together, but at the end of summer, Barack had to return to Harvard – more than 800 miles away – where he had two more years of law school to complete. Michelle continued working at the law firm of Sidley & Austin. The couple began a long-distance relationship of telephone calls and letters.

Although it was difficult for them to be so far apart, they remained committed to each other.

Barack and Michelle got together for weekend visits in Boston or Chicago as often as they could.

Would the relationship survive the two years they had to be apart?

# CHAPTER SEVEN

## 'If what you're doing doesn't bring you joy every single day, what's the point?'

In 1991, Michelle received shocking news. Her father, who had recently undergone kidney surgery, had collapsed and died while on his way to work. Fraser Robinson was 55 years old, his daughter 27. Despite her worry about his health due to the multiple sclerosis, Michelle was taken by surprise by her father's sudden death. It caused her a deep sense of loss.

Fraser's death came after another momentous event in Michelle's life. Her room-mate at Princeton, Suzanne Alele, had died four months after she was diagnosed with cancer. Michelle was at her bedside when she passed away. Michelle had long admired Suzanne. She often told Michelle to relax more and not worry so much about her career. At her funeral, Michelle reflected on what Suzanne had said. If she herself should die in four months' time, she wondered, would she have spent the time she had in the best way possible?

The passing of both her father and Suzanne caused Michelle to ask herself some hard questions. She wondered if she had chosen the right career path or had simply climbed onto the 'automatic path' of a corporate career. She began thinking about how she had gone to some of the best schools and colleges in the country, yet still didn't really know what she wanted to do. She thought about how her education allowed her to make a good living, yet she felt she wasn't learning anything about the world, giving anything back or finding her passion and then letting that guide her. It shouldn't, she realized, be all about what kind of college she had gone to.

It was time for a change.

When Michelle told her bosses at Sidley & Austin that she was going to leave, they tried to discourage her. They said she had a wonderful future at the law firm. But Michelle knew – in her heart, where it mattered – that she was making the right decision. She had no specific job in mind, however, and now began looking at various options for a career in public service. This included working in the offices of Chicago Mayor Richard M. Daley.

The mayor was the son of the former Mayor Daley, who had headed the Democratic political machine when Michelle had been a young girl, helping her father knock on doors for the Democrats. Michelle knew that the former mayor had opposed Revd King's marches and had tried to keep black Chicagoans segregated, so she was worried about working for his son. But Michelle established an instant rapport with Valerie Jarrett, a top aide to the mayor.

## FACT FILE

Valerie Jarrett, who hired Michelle for her first public service job, was not an old-style Chicago politician. The deputy chief of staff to Mayor Daley was from a distinguished black family whose grandfather and father had broken barriers for African Americans. Born in Iran where her physician father ran a children's hospital, Jarrett was a lawyer who devoted herself to public service. Jarrett became a senior advisor to President Obama and now works at the White House. Valerie Jarrett was one of many contacts Michelle made who would help Barack on his path to the presidency.

Jarrett was impressed with the young lawyer. A brief scheduled interview turned into a wide-ranging hour and a half discussion, which ended with Jarrett offering Michelle a job.

Michelle was put in charge of helping businesses expand in Chicago. While she lacked experience in this area, she used the business knowledge she had acquired at the law firm to act as a trouble-shooter. She quickly earned a reputation as a problem solver, and as someone who was 'totally unflappable', as a colleague later reported.

During this time, Michelle and Barack started talking about marriage. They had been together for three years and Michelle wanted to get married. But Barack doubted whether marriage was really necessary: *he* thought that marriage in itself didn't really mean anything and that what was important was how the two of them felt about each other. This caused some friction between them. Michelle finally told him that she wasn't prepared to just 'hang out forever' – she wanted the commitment of marriage.

Later that year, Barack finally graduated from

Harvard Law School and passed the bar exam, which allowed him to practise law in Illinois.

He could now work in Chicago and be with Michelle.

It was time for another big step.

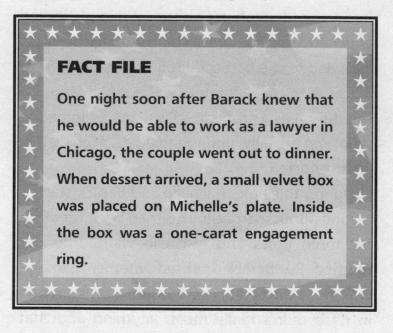

**FACT FILE**

One night soon after Barack knew that he would be able to work as a lawyer in Chicago, the couple went out to dinner. When dessert arrived, a small velvet box was placed on Michelle's plate. Inside the box was a one-carat engagement ring.

# CHAPTER EIGHT

## 'We know we are blessed.'

Michelle and Barack were married on 18 October 1992 at Trinity United Church of Christ on Chicago's South Side. Michelle was 28 years old and Barack was 31. The couple honeymooned in California and returned to live in Chicago where Barack had been spearheading a voter registration drive for the 1992 presidential election.

Michelle got a job as director of Public Allies: an organization that trained 18 to 30 year olds who wanted to pursue careers in public service. More than fifteen years later, as First Lady, Michelle recalled that she was never happier than when she was just married and was working at Public Allies. This was the first job that had been hers to develop, and it combined her passions with her talents.

Her work ranged from canvassing door-to-door in some of Chicago's poorest neighbourhoods to arranging fundraising events with the city's professional elite. She used the contacts she had made at Sidley & Austin and the mayor's office to attract college students to the programme.

Julian Posada, the assistant director, recalled how, as a result of Michelle's efforts, they got students from what he described as a 'very lily-white campus' to sit down alongside inner-city kids from diverse backgrounds – black, Hispanic and Asian. He was impressed by Michelle's attention to detail combined with her courtesy to both staff and volunteers. Nothing was 'beneath' her, he told journalist Liza Mundy, and she was prepared to do whatever was necessary to get the job done – even stuffing and licking envelopes! She didn't treat the organization like a plush law firm at all.

Michelle in fact became very instrumental in showing minority kids that the American dream was attainable.

'She was the first person I met who came from a similar, working-class background to mine, who was able to make it both in academic life and professional life and who said you can get the skill-set and learn as much as you can, and still give back to your community,' said Jose Rico, a young immigrant from Mexico who worked with Michelle.

The need to make a difference in the lives of others was one she shared with her husband. His work on the voter registration drive had whetted his political aspirations, and he was elected to the Illinois Senate in 1996.

This meant he now represented a large portion of the South Side in the state government.

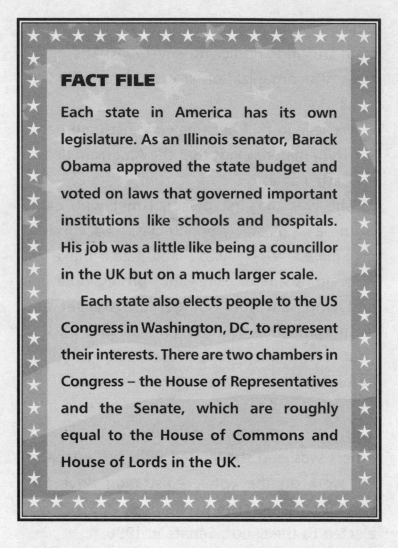

Michelle had mixed emotions over her husband's election. For one thing, it meant that they would be separated for days at a time when the Illinois legislature, located 200 miles away in Springfield, was in session. Going into politics also meant that Barack would sacrifice the possibility of a good salary as a private lawyer.

After much thought and debate, Michelle not only backed his decision, but played a valuable role in advancing her husband's political career. Being a native of Chicago, she knew many more people than he did. So as he got more involved in politics, she was able to help him solidify his relationships with key people and steer him in the right direction.

**FACT FILE**

Michelle played an integral role in the Obama household. As a corporate lawyer and senior public servant, she earned more than her husband, and helped to finance his political career.

# CHAPTER NINE

*'Every other month since I've had children, I've struggled with the notion of "Am I being a good parent? Can I stay at home? Should I stay home? How do I balance it all"?'*

Michelle and Barack decided it was time to start a family.

Hoping to be the best mother she could, Michelle realized that her commitment to her job at Public Allies would pose a conflict. She found a replacement to head up the organization, then started looking for part-time work so she would be available to her children, just like her mother had been to her.

Based on her experience of encouraging young people to aim for careers in public service, she was hired by the University of Chicago to put together a similar programme for its students.

Although it was located only a short distance from her childhood home, the University of Chicago had a reputation for being aloof from the community around it. Michelle herself certainly remembered that, as a kid growing up on the South Side, she had thought of the University of Chicago as something akin to a foreign country. But the university wanted to change. Uniquely positioned to bridge the gap between 'town and gown', Michelle used her skills to develop the university's well-regarded Community Service Centre.

But her life was changing in other ways. On 4 July 1998, Independence Day in America – a national holiday – Michelle gave birth to a daughter, Malia Ann. Malia means 'queen' in Swahili, and Ann was the name of Barack's mother.

Michelle and Barack were now parents.

> 'The Barack Obama I know today is the same man I fell in love with nineteen years ago. He's the same man who drove me and our new baby daughter home from the hospital ten years ago this summer, inching along at a snail's pace, peering anxiously at us in the rearview mirror, feeling the whole weight of her future in his hands.'
>
> *Michelle Obama, August 2008*

Having a child to care for put a definite strain on the couple's marriage. Barack had his job in Springfield and, in addition, was teaching a course at the University of Chicago Law School. Michelle was left to care for the family and household on her own. She became so angry at her husband's absences that she could barely speak to him on a family holiday in Hawaii. When she did finally have her say, she accused him of thinking only of himself. They had decided together to have children, yet now she found herself raising their daughter virtually alone. It wasn't what she had thought would happen.

Michelle's words stung Barack, but they served as a wake-up call for both of them. He realized how one-sided their relationship had become and made a concerted effort to spend more time with his family. Michelle realized she couldn't change his workaholic nature, but she could make sure that he helped with the family more when he was at home.

This is still the case today! Even though her husband is the US President, Michelle insists that Barack stay involved in family affairs, and he makes sure he spends time with his children as much as he can.

By the time their second daughter, Natasha (nicknamed Sasha) was born in 2001, the couple had worked out a system that better balanced the demands of work and family life. Always an early riser, Michelle got to work early and left Barack to care for the girls at breakfast. They hired a housekeeper to cook, clean and do the laundry while Michelle's mother Marian, who lived nearby, helped with the babysitting. Just as Barack had a close relationship with his grandparents, and Michelle had had regular contact with her grandparents, Michelle's mother was now involved in the lives of her two grandchildren.

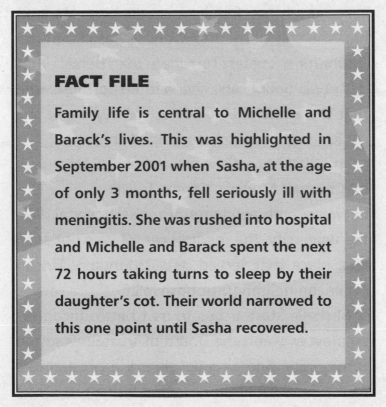

### FACT FILE

Family life is central to Michelle and Barack's lives. This was highlighted in September 2001 when Sasha, at the age of only 3 months, fell seriously ill with meningitis. She was rushed into hospital and Michelle and Barack spent the next 72 hours taking turns to sleep by their daughter's cot. Their world narrowed to this one point until Sasha recovered.

Once Michelle started to look at her circumstances differently and set up a support structure, she became more understanding and accepting of her husband. Rather than looking to Barack to give her all the answers or to help her feel fulfilled, she realized that she needed to focus on what worked for her and kept her 'sane'.

Although her family was very important to her, she still wanted to work towards a better future for those less fortunate than herself. And with two daughters, she wanted to make sure that the world they grew up into was one she could feel proud to have helped shape.

In 2002, Michelle was hired by the University of Chicago Medical Center to serve as a go-between with residents near the hospital. Like the university, the medical centre was not seen as a place that served its surrounding African American neighbourhoods well.

Michelle started bus tours to introduce new employees – and the board of trustees – to the community. She also developed a programme to send doctors into community hospitals and clinics, while educating residents about the importance of preventative care and regular medical check-ups.

Michelle had expected that her husband would leave politics when he had served his term as a state senator. Instead, with the US Senate seat up for grabs in Illinois, Barack told her of his desire to run for the position, which would make him one of two senators who represented Illinois in Washington. It was a daring move that at first filled Michelle with worry. The odds of winning were stacked against her husband. But Michelle knew from the day she first met him at Sidley & Austin that Barack was a man with high ambitions. She gave him her full support – although she qualified it with the joke that maybe he'd lose.

Barack won by a landslide, becoming only the fifth African American in history to become a US senator.

When he was sworn in at the Capitol building in Washington in January 2005, Michelle and the girls were at his side. After the ceremony, the Obamas stepped outside the building for a breath of fresh air. Barack's victory had turned him into a much-talked-about public figure, and the family was trailed by the media. Six-year-old Malia took one look at the microphones and cameras following them and asked her father a question: was he going to be the President?

It would take another four years before Malia got her answer.

# CHAPTER TEN

*'She is smart, funny, and thoroughly charming. If I ever had to run against her for public office, she would beat me without too much difficulty.'* **Barack Obama**

Barack Obama's campaign for the US Senate not only tested his appeal to voters in a state with a majority white population, but it also offered valuable lessons to Michelle on the art of campaigning.

The time-honoured role for candidate's wives is to be seen but not heard. This was not acceptable to Michelle. If she was going to help Barack in his Senate race, she was going to do more than provide dutiful head nods. She began to write her own speeches and campaign for her husband on her own. She marshalled her considerable communication skills to talk about problems facing average families, such as rising health-care costs, and explain in detail how Barack was committed to helping them.

Her ability to connect directly with voters through her empathy and straight talk turned out to be a great asset to Barack's Senate campaign. She became his so-called 'secret weapon' because her presence in small Illinois towns and many Chicago neighbourhoods gave him a chance to meet nearly twice as many voters.

The campaign got even more hectic after Barack was asked to deliver the keynote address at the 2004 Democratic National Convention during the middle of his Senate race. The all-important address would be heard and watched by millions of people all over the world. The 5,000 delegates would be the largest crowd that Barack had ever addressed.

Before he delivered the speech, he rehearsed it in front of Michelle. She had always been his toughest critic, and Barack knew that she could be brutally honest. Later, he told reporters how she had come into the practice room and after listening to his rehearsal, she had announced that she didn't think he was going to embarrass the Obama family.

As the time neared for Barack to deliver the keynote address, Michelle saw that her usually unflappable husband was getting nervous. She waited until just before Barack strode onto the stage to calm him down. She leaned in close and said, 'Just don't screw it up, buddy.'

It worked. Barack laughed and then went out to give an outstanding speech that brought the house down. His speech was widely regarded as electrifying. It instantly placed Obama on the national stage as a major political figure.

A life-altering decision was coming.

Over the next two years, as Barack's political star continued to rise as a US Senator, prominent Democrats began urging him to run for the presidency in 2008.

Barack made it clear that he would not consider becoming a presidential candidate

## FACT FILE

The presidential election is a battle between a candidate representing the Democratic Party and a candidate representing the Republican Party. (There are other US political parties, but they win few votes.) Candidates first have to be chosen by their party. This involves campaigning across America and holding primary elections, where party members vote for delegates to represent the candidates of their choice. Barack Obama needed to win more delegates than several other rivals to become the Democratic Party's nominee for president. His strongest challenger was Hillary Clinton, wife of former President Bill Clinton, who was the first female candidate for the Democrats.

unless Michelle was 100% behind him. In his view, Michelle had veto power over decisions that had a direct impact on their family.

David Axelrod, Obama's chief political strategist, said Michelle peppered him with many practical questions about a presidential run, especially the potential impact it might have on their young children, Malia and Sasha.

Ever the well-prepared lawyer, Michelle also held meetings with Barack's staff to make sure the campaign would be run efficiently. She conferred with campaign donors to be make sure they would back his candidacy.

Ultimately, she concluded that the promise of bringing historic change to America was worth the risks and personal hardships. Typically, she downplayed her role, humorously telling her audiences that she told Barack he could run for the presidency during a family vacation in Hawaii. After all, when you're in Hawaii on a beach, everything looks possible.

On 10 February 2007, before a cheering crowd in Springfield, Illinois, Barack Obama announced his candidacy. With Michelle at his side, he introduced the phrase that would become his campaign's rallying call: 'Yes We Can.'

Now he needed to hit the campaign trail and win Democratic votes throughout the whole country.

# CHAPTER ELEVEN

*'There is so much at stake in this election. The direction of our country hangs in the balance. We are faced with two clear choices: The world as it is, and the world as it should be.'*

For Michelle, her husband's campaign became a complex juggling act. At first, she left the details of the campaign to Barack and his staff and focused her attention on keeping life as normal as possible for Malia and Sasha. But great changes were in store for them. The point was driven home when Secret Service agents were assigned to their Chicago home to protect them.

Michelle told *Newsweek* magazine that

this was 'the first sign that our lives aren't normal'. Fortunately, Malia and Sasha took the intrusion of the stony-faced agents in their stride and began calling them the 'secret people'.

Hillary Clinton was far ahead of Barack in the early polls. Recalling her role in his US Senate race, the Obama organization thought that Michelle could be a powerful advocate for her husband, especially before female audiences. They were right.

When introducing Barack on the 'stump', or during a campaign stop, Michelle impressed crowds with her humorous delivery and down-to-earth nature. Journalists agreed that her easy approach complemented Barack's more intellectual style, while underlining the same message of hope and change. Her presence on the stage, moreover, was of obvious pleasure to her husband.

Her special appeal was to female audiences. Writing her own speeches, she not only discussed the lack of child-care facilities, but how to improve education, how to break down racial barriers, and how to strengthen family life. These were all issues that had absorbed her ever since she had abandoned her corporate career.

'I'm here not just because I'm the wife of a candidate,' she told one group. 'I'm here as a woman, as a mother, as a citizen of this country. And I'm so tired of the way things are.'

As the campaign continued, she made arrangements to travel to political events that kept disruption of her family to a minimum. She limited travel to day trips and would travel overnight only if her daughters could come along.

A typical campaign day could be exhausting. She would get on a plane, go to a city, do several events, then get back on the plane and be home before her children's bedtime. She matter-of-factly described herself as being a little tired at the end of such a day – but as far as her daughters were concerned, 'Mommy' had just been at work.

The first stage of the presidential campaign was more than halfway over when, in February 2008, Michelle told a crowd in Milwaukee, Wisconsin: 'For the first time in my adult life, I am proud of my country because it feels like hope is finally making a comeback.' Later that evening, she re-worded her speech at another campaign stop, saying, 'For the first time in my adult lifetime, I'm really proud of my country. And not just because Barack has done well, but because I think people are hungry for change.'

Many conservative commentators pounced upon Michelle's statement, quoting only the first part of what she said. Cindy McCain, the wife of John McCain, the leading nominee for the Republican Party, lost no time criticizing Michelle by saying, 'I've *always* been proud of my country.' Her husband's opponents tried to portray Michelle as an unpatriotic and angry black woman, with one conservative magazine mocking her as 'Mrs Grievance'.

Michelle explained that she was commenting only on the state of politics, not on her love for the country. But for people who wanted to view the Obamas as 'anti-American', her comment was recycled endlessly in the media. One video ad paid for by the Tennessee Republican Party showed various people giving different reasons why they were proud of America while a voiceover kept repeating Michelle's words.

Michelle was hurt by these unfounded attacks, but she kept on campaigning for Barack and for the principles in which she believed. In a televised interview with talk-show host Larry King, she was asked directly about the impact of race on the campaign. She replied, 'The thing that I've always found and what makes me hopeful, especially when I travel around places like Iowa and places where there are not that many black folks, is that where I connect with people is around values. It's around the stories of my upbringing, growing up in a working-class background.'

Most voters, she went on to say, wanted to discuss issues that went beyond race and partisan bickering. 'The notion that you treat people with decency and respect even if you don't always agree with them or don't know them – you know, people hear that. And it reminds them of who they are and who they hope to be. And that transcends race.'

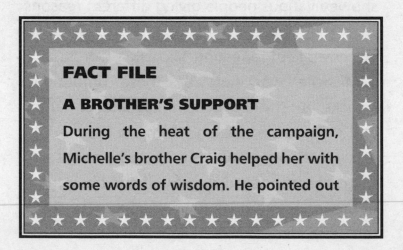

**FACT FILE**

**A BROTHER'S SUPPORT**

During the heat of the campaign, Michelle's brother Craig helped her with some words of wisdom. He pointed out that a presidential election was a lot like a game of basketball: should the team be down, they might try everything they could to get back in the game, even if it involved using their elbows or fouling their opponent. Politics, in his view, was very much the same.

Craig had returned to basketball in 1999 after giving up a career as a successful investment banker. He was an assistant coach at Northwestern University near Chicago for six years before he became head coach at Brown University in 2006. The Brown Bears finished the 2007-08 season second in the league with a team record of 19 wins. In April 2008, he was named head basketball coach at Oregon State University.

The attacks on Michelle eventually proved to be ineffective. As people began to look at her more closely, a large number of them liked what they saw. She got the nickname of 'The Closer' because she had persuaded so many people to vote for her husband in the primary campaign.

As Hillary Clinton admitted defeat and urged her Democratic supporters to back Barack Obama, Michelle's husband became the official presidential candidate for the Democratic Party – the first African American ever to win the nomination of a major party. He would be running against Republican John McCain.

# CHAPTER TWELVE

*'She's beautifully dressed without too much fuss. She puts on the dress and goes – and it's always a good dress.'*

Unusual things happen in the glare of presidential campaigns where candidates and their wives are closely scrutinized. In Michelle's case, it was the public's discovery of her fashion sense. A careful and imaginative dresser since childhood, she became a trendsetter on the campaign trail.

Her smart and affordable ensembles became the much-talked-about sensation of the otherwise serious Obama campaign.

An off-the-rack dress that Michelle wore on morning television show, *The View*, was so admired that every look-alike dress flew off the hangers of the chain store. It was a sleeveless black and white sundress that cost only about $170.

Michelle typically wore pieces from lesser-known American designers that cost a fraction of the cost of the couture designer suits worn by the wives of other candidates.

One fashion consultant in New York, Tom Julian, credited Michelle with changing America's fashion tastes by wearing both high-end and low-end clothes – her choices helped to bring affordable American sportswear to the forefront, which he stated was very appealing to the Middle American woman voter. Both *People* and *Vanity Fair* magazines listed Michelle among the world's best-dressed people.

What was striking about Michelle's elevation to fashion icon was that her style was completely her own. She did not use a stylist and did not hire others to buy her clothes. When asked what

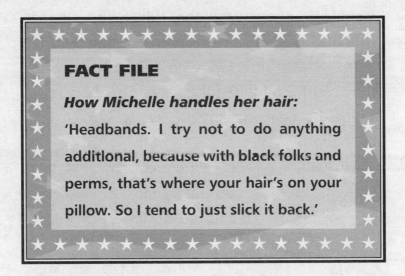

**FACT FILE**

*How Michelle handles her hair:*
'Headbands. I try not to do anything additional, because with black folks and perms, that's where your hair's on your pillow. So I tend to just slick it back.'

her fashion secret was, she simply stated that she thought women should wear what they liked.

Some of her fashion trademarks became the sleeveless classic shift dress, low-heeled pointed flats, and small colour-coordinated cardigans. When she wore sleeves, they were often billowy. Her ensembles were typically accessorized with a string or two of pearls and a few well-chosen pieces of jewellery. Because her hair is thick, she often styled it in a flipped bob.

It didn't take long before people started comparing her fashion influence to that of

Jacqueline Kennedy in the 1960s, the elegant wife of the late President John F. Kennedy.

The South Side girl who had once joyfully shown off a new handbag was now becoming a global style icon.

# CHAPTER THIRTEEN

*'I come here as a wife who loves my husband and believes he will be an extraordinary president.'*

On the night of 25 August 2008, as Barack Obama celebrated the fact that he had won the Democratic Party's nomination for President, he asked Michelle to introduce him to the thousands of jubilant supporters at the party's national convention in Denver, Colorado.

She spoke of the 'improbable journey' that brought her and her husband to this historic occasion, 'where a girl from the South Side of Chicago can go to college and law school, and the son of a single mother from Hawaii can go all the way to the White House.'

She explained how her own life story was an example of the aspirations shared by many Americans. Sounding a theme that would be repeated in the final two months of the campaign, Michelle referred to hope, not fear, as the motivation of the Obama campaign. 'We want our children – and all children in this nation – to know that the only limit to the height of your achievements is the reach of your dreams and your willingness to work for them.'

The crowd responded with wild cheers.

It was this straightforward and charismatic Michelle that won over the American public. If Barack was the brains of the final dash to the presidency – those two concentrated months of campaigning in the autumn of 2008 – Michelle assumed the vital role of the heart. Speaking tirelessly before audiences around the country, she redoubled her efforts as 'The Closer' to state the case for her husband.

On Election Day, 4 November 2008, Barack Obama clinched a decisive victory.

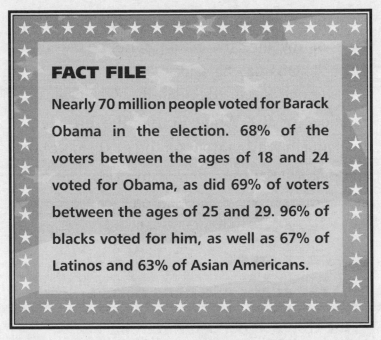

That evening the Obama family gathered with friends and relatives at the Hyatt Regency Hotel in Chicago to watch the election results. After the network news channels announced his big win, the Obama family went to Chicago's Grant Park, where 100,000 people had converged to celebrate. Thanking his supporters, Barack Obama saved the greatest praise for his wife:

'I would not be standing here tonight without the unyielding support of my best friend for the last 16 years, the rock of our family, the love of my life, the nation's next First Lady, Michelle Obama,' he said.

The great-great-granddaughter of slaves was headed for the White House, the president's mansion in Washington, on the next stop of her improbable journey.

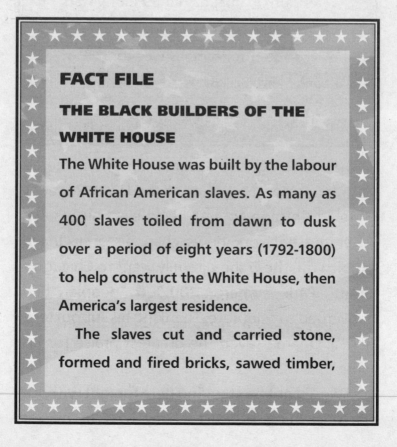

**FACT FILE**

**THE BLACK BUILDERS OF THE WHITE HOUSE**

The White House was built by the labour of African American slaves. As many as 400 slaves toiled from dawn to dusk over a period of eight years (1792-1800) to help construct the White House, then America's largest residence.

The slaves cut and carried stone, formed and fired bricks, sawed timber, made plaster moulds and did a lot of the carpentry. They worked alongside about 200 free black and white workmen.

Pierre L'Enfant, who designed and planned the city of Washington, DC, contracted with slave owners to use their slaves to dig the foundations of the White House. James Hoban, architect of the White House, brought some of his own slaves from South Carolina to work on the building. Slave owners received $5 per slave each month from the government. In return, the slaves worked six, and sometimes seven, days a week from sun-up to sun-down.

Two months later – on 20 January 2009, just three days after Michelle's 45th birthday – Michelle and her daughters stood on the steps of the US Capitol building as her husband took the Presidential Oath of Office in front of nearly 2 million people gathered in the National Mall, a park that stretches for more than a mile from the Capitol building to the Lincoln Memorial.

# CHAPTER FOURTEEN

*'My first job in all honesty is going to continue to be mom-in-chief.'*

The White House at 1600 Pennsylvania Avenue, Washington, DC, has four floors and 54 rooms. The ground and first floors are open to the public and for official state functions. The second and third floors are the family's living quarters. Michelle wasted no time making sure that her family made a smooth transition to their new living space after her husband was sworn in as America's 44th president in January 2009.

Before the move, Michelle convinced her 71-year-old mother to relocate from her small home in Chicago to the White House. She felt that the girls needed her as part of their sense of stability.

Marian agreed, telling a reporter humorously: 'I'll be mad, but I'll do it.' Her presence in the White House marks the first time in decades that three generations of a presidential family have settled into the mansion.

Michelle decorated the girls' bedrooms with items that made them feel at home and comfortable. But the White House is a museum full of famous artefacts as well as a private home, so when Malia does her homework, she can sit at the desk where President Abraham Lincoln wrote the Emancipation Proclamation that freed black slaves in 1863.

Although Malia and Sasha live in a mansion with its own movie theatre, bowling alley, and a huge staff of attendants, the girls still have to make their own beds and clean their own rooms.

**FACT FILE**

Other house rules transferred from Chicago to the White House were:

- No whining, arguing or annoying teasing.
- Set your own alarm clock and dress yourself in the morning.
- Keep your playroom toy closet clean.
- No more than one hour of television watching per night.

One of the best aspects of living in the mansion is that the family can be together. 'It means that we see each other every day . . . just to be able to have the casual conversations that happen about life at dinner time,' said Michelle.

President Obama enjoys taking what he calls 'Michelle time' at the Oval Office, his official workspace at the White House. Every now and again, Michelle shows up at the Oval Office with the girls for a brief but lively interruption. Michelle has said that if the kids really need to see him, they can. It's important to both of them that they are free to walk into the Oval Office.

One year into her unpaid job as mistress of the White House, Michelle Obama has been the most active First Lady in recent history. She has taken on various community and political projects, touring soup kitchens in Washington, pushing for her husband's economic stimulus package, and making an unexpectedly strong commitment to the local Washington community. Typical of the events she regularly hosts was an afternoon of music for 180 sixth and seventh graders from a Washington state school as part of a celebration of African American History Month.

Dressed in a crisp white shirt, green sweater and tweed skirt, she gave the kids a short history lesson touching on several black history milestones at the White House. She explained that the White House had been built, in part, by slaves and that Dr Martin Luther King Jr and other civil rights leaders had come there to meet with past presidents.

She asked the kids, 'Who lives here now?'

'President Obama,' they answered in unison.

'President Obama. And he's making history every single day. Why?'

'He's the first African American president of the United States,' one little girl said.

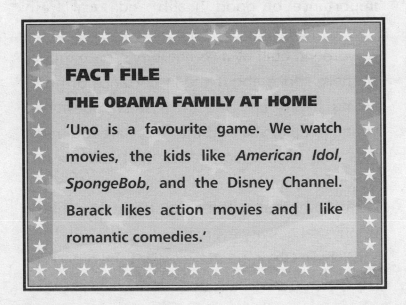

**FACT FILE**

**THE OBAMA FAMILY AT HOME**

'Uno is a favourite game. We watch movies, the kids like *American Idol*, *SpongeBob*, and the Disney Channel. Barack likes action movies and I like romantic comedies.'

Students from another school visited the White House to harvest the organic vegetable garden that they had grown under the First Lady's supervision. The organic garden not only will provide food for the first family's meals, but will be used for formal state dinners. 'The planting of this garden was one of the first things I wanted to do as First Lady at the White House,' she told the students. 'You helped make this dream a reality.'

The garden project was part of her broader plan to bring national attention to the importance of good health and local fresh foods. Speaking at the dedication of a playground built by a community service group, Michelle spoke about the importance of good eating habits and the increase of obesity in young people. She said that there are too many kids who have a high-calorie diet and are not getting enough exercise. In order to stay healthy, she believes that children should get 60 minutes of physical activity every day.

Michelle Obama practices what she preaches. On a typical day, she gets up at 5:30 a.m. to work out in order to stay in good physical shape. Her physical trainer Cornell McClellan has said that Michelle often does a hardcore cardio and resistance session, followed by an arm-shaping superset involving tricep pushdowns and hammer curls using dumbbells.

Michelle insists on a diet of organic and natural foods for herself and her family. She says that her emphasis on healthy foods came from her experiences as a busy mother trying to feed her daughters. Eating out three times a week, ordering a pizza, having a sandwich for dinner all took their toll and the girls began to put on weight, which wasn't healthy for them. Her paediatrician told her she needed to be thinking more about nutrition and Michelle listened. Within months the girls had lost the extra weight.

Michelle Obama's new role as 'mom-in-chief' has only just begun. She has instructed those who work for her to think carefully because she wants everything she says and does in public to connect to the lives of working families. She has been involved in the president's health-care reform plan. She has also started an advisory board to help families with loved ones in the military service.

As a role model and advocate for families and children, Michelle Obama is creating positive change and setting higher standards and expectations for women everywhere. Her goals during her husband's term as president are perhaps best summed up in her own words, delivered to graduating seniors at the University of California-Merced in May 2009:

'Dream big, think broadly about your life, and please make giving back to your community a part of that vision. Take the same hope and optimism, the hard work and tenacity that brought you to this point, and carry that with you for the rest of your life in whatever you choose to do.'

'The next chapter in
history is written by you.
That's not just a story that
Barack Obama is writing . . .
Those are the stories that
we're all writing together,
and you're an important
part of that.'

*Michelle Obama*

# EQUALITY OF OPPORTUNITY

*'I'm so happy that my girls will grow up where the prospect of a woman or African American president is normal . . . I want them to grow up in a world where they don't have to limit themselves, where they can dream and achieve without ever hitting a glass ceiling.'*

Equality of opportunity is very important for both Barack and Michelle Obama. Here are some of the key moments leading up to, and during, Michelle's lifetime which have helped enable ambitious women to reach for their goals. For women from non-white backgrounds who live in white majority countries like the US, the struggle has been twice as hard, as equality legislation has also been needed to reduce discrimination due to skin colour.

★ **1955:** A black seamstress called Rosa Parks refuses to give up her seat to a white man on a bus in Alabama. Her actions spark a series of peaceful protests, culminating in the Civil Rights Movement.

★ **1961:** President Kennedy highlights women's rights, and investigates ideas such as paid maternity leave and affordable childcare.

★ **1963:** The Equal Pay Act in the US prohibits employers from paying men and women differently for the same job. It took about 20 years for this law to be passed after it was first proposed.

★ Soviet cosmonaut Valentina Tereshkova becomes the first woman in space.

★ **1964:** Michelle LaVaughn Robinson born.
★ The Civil Rights Act in US bars employment discrimination based on race and gender.

★ **1967:** Marriage between people of different races becomes legal throughout the USA.

★ **1968:** Shirley Chisholm becomes the first African American woman elected to the US Congress. She later runs for President.

★ **1973:** Female tennis player Billy Jean King beats male tennis star Bobby Riggs in 'The Battle of the Sexes': an enormous victory for women's sport.

★ **1978:** More women than men enter university in America for the first time.

★ **1979:** Margaret Thatcher elected as the first female Prime Minister of the UK.

* **1981:** Sandra Day O'Connor is the first woman ever appointed to the US Supreme Court.

* **1986:** The first broadcast of the *Oprah Winfrey Show* on US TV. Oprah would later become referred to as the most influential woman in the world.

* **1988:** At 18, Naomi Campbell is the first black female to appear on the cover of French *Vogue*. It launches her career as a supermodel.

* **1993:** Toni Morrison becomes the first African American woman to win the Nobel Prize for Literature.

* **1994:** The first female priests are ordained in the Church of England.

* **1997:** Madeline Albright is sworn in as the first female Secretary of State under President Bill Clinton. This is the highest political role that a woman has ever occupied in the US.

★ **2002:** Halle Berry becomes the first African American woman to win an Oscar.

★ A change to the Employment Act in the UK allows parents with young children more flexible working hours.

★ **2003:** Baroness Amos becomes the first black woman in the UK Cabinet.

★ **2005:** Condoleeza Rice becomes Secretary of State under President George W. Bush.

★ **2007:** Hillary Clinton announces her candidacy for the Democratic nomination for the presidency.

★ **2009:** Ursula Burns becomes the first African American woman to be CEO of a Fortune 500 company. The Fortune 500 is a list of the richest American businesses.

★ Barack Obama is inaugurated as the first African American President of the US; Michelle becomes First Lady.

## Some inspiring women who have aimed high and achieved their goals:

### ★ ★ ★ Baroness Valerie Amos ★ ★ ★

Baroness Amos was born in Guyana in 1954. She became Chief Executive of the Equal Opportunities Commission in 1989, was joint first black woman peer (1997), the first black woman to become Leader of the House of Lords (2003) and the first black female Cabinet minister (2003). She now works in finance.

### ★ ★ ★ Malorie Blackman, OBE ★ ★ ★

Malorie is an award-winning author of over 50 books for children and young adults. In 2005, Malorie was honoured with the Eleanor Farjeon Award in recognition of her distinguished contribution to the world of children's books.

### ★ ★ ★ Carol Moseley Braun ★ ★ ★

Carol is currently the only African American woman ever to have served in the United States Senate. She served in national government from 1993–1999.

## ★ ★ ★ Shirley Chisholm ★ ★ ★

Shirley was born in New York to Caribbean parents. She held a political post in Congress for several years. Despite what she called 'impossible odds', she later ran for President, to show that she wanted to see change in politics.

## ★ ★ ★ Chinwe Chukwuogo-Roy ★ ★ ★

Chinwe is an artist of Nigerian origin who moved to the UK in 1975. Her work is exhibited all over the world. She was invited to paint a portrait of Queen Elizabeth II in 2002.

## ★ ★ ★ Hillary Clinton ★ ★ ★

Born in 1947, Hillary was active in political activities from a young age. Her husband Bill Clinton became the US President in 1992. Hillary ran for the Democratic Party nomination for President in 2008 but conceded victory to Obama. She became Secretary of State in Obama's government.

## ★ ★ ★ Kanya King, MBE ★ ★ ★

Kanya King is the founder and CEO of the MOBO awards, which celebrate music of black origin, showcasing talent from all over the world. Kanya worked to set up and run the show, which has been going since 1996. The ceremony is now broadcast worldwide.

## ★ ★ ★ Doreen Lawrence ★ ★ ★

Since her son Stephen Lawrence was murdered in 1993, Doreen has campaigned on social justice issues. Through her work, major changes have been made to the police and public services to decrease racial discrimination. She launched the Stephen Lawrence Charitable Trust and, in 2008, opened the Stephen Lawrence Centre in London.

## ★ ★ ★ Penny McDonald ★ ★ ★

Penny was the first black journalist on the *Telegraph* newspaper, where she worked for 13 years. She is now the managing director of a PR firm, with clients including Rihanna, Amy Winehouse and ex-Beatle Sir Paul McCartney.

### ★ ★ ★ Angela Merkel ★ ★ ★

Angela is the Chancellor of Germany, a powerful head of state. She is the first woman to have held this post. She was successfully re-elected leader in 2009.

### ★ ★ ★ Dr Uchenna Okoye ★ ★ ★

Nigerian-born Uchenna is a leading cosmetic dentist in the UK. She owns two surgeries and is the resident dentist on the popular TV show *Ten Years Younger*.

### ★ ★ ★ Elsie Owusu ★ ★ ★

Elsie is an architect who has worked on projects in west Africa, Europe and the Middle East. She is the founder of the Society of Black Architects. Her most recent work includes the design for the new UK Supreme Court building.

### ★ ★ ★ Condoleeza Rice ★ ★ ★

Condoleeza Rice became adviser to the US President George W. Bush on foreign affairs and national security in 2005. She remains the most powerful black woman in US political history.

## ★ ★ ★ Lady Margaret Thatcher ★ ★ ★

Lady Thatcher is the daughter of a greengrocer from Lincolnshire. She became an MP in 1959, then the Conservative Party leader. She was the first female Prime Minister of the UK and held power from 1979–1992.

## ★ ★ ★ Samantha Tross ★ ★ ★

Samantha is an orthopaedic surgeon. There are few female doctors in this area of medicine.

## ★ ★ ★ Madame C.J. Walker ★ ★ ★

Born as Sarah Breedlove in 1868, Madame Walker was the first in her family to be born free after the Emancipation of slaves. She successfully developed hair care and cosmetic products for black women. Madame Walker became the first self-made female millionaire.

## ★ ★ ★ Verna Wilkins ★ ★ ★

Verna was born in Grenada and lives in London. She founded the publishing company, Tamarind Books in 1987. She won the British Book Industry Award for Cultural Diversity in 2008.

## ★ ★ ★  Oprah Winfrey  ★ ★ ★

Oprah is the first African American woman billionaire and first African American woman to host a nationally-broadcast talk show. She is also an actress and was nominated for an Oscar for her role in the film *The Color Purple*.

## ★  Baroness Margaret Omolola Young  ★

Baroness Lola Young has held senior positions in several arts organizations, including the Royal National Theatre and the South Bank Centre. She was made a peer in 2004 and votes in the House of Lords.

# FURTHER READING

For more information on Michelle Obama, you can visit the White House website:

**www.whitehouse.gov**

For more information on Black History in Britain:

**www.bbc.co.uk/1xtra/blackhistory**

**www.blackhistorymonthuk.co.uk**

For more information about your personal rights:

**www.equalityhumanrights.com**

The Equality and Human Rights Commission in Britain was formed in October 2007, and builds on the legacies of the Equal Opportunities Commission, the Commission for Racial Equality and the Disability Rights Commission to work towards the elimination of all discrimination, reduce inequality, protect human rights and build good relations, ensuring that everyone has a fair chance in life.

# BIBLIOGRAPHY

## Books and Monographs

Allen, William C., 'History of Slave Laborers in the Construction of the United States Capitol.' Washington, DC: 1 June 2005.

Brophy, David Bergen. *Michelle Obama: Meet the First Lady*. New York: Collins, 2009.

Colbert, David. *Michelle Obama: An American Story*. Boston: Houghton Mifflin, 2009.

Lightfoot, Elizabeth. *Michelle Obama: First Lady of Hope*. Guilford, Connecticut: Lyons Press, 2009.

Mundy, Liza. *Michelle, A Biography*. New York: Simon & Schuster, 2008.

Obama, Barack. *Dreams from My Father: A Story of Race and Inheritance*. New York: Random House, 1995, 2004; UK: Canongate Books, 2007.

Obama, Barack. *The Audacity of Hope: Thoughts on Reclaiming the American Dream*. New York: Crown, 2006.

Obama, Michelle, 'Princeton-Educated Blacks and the Black Community.' Princeton, N.J.: 1985.

Rogak, Lisa (ed.). *Michelle Obama in her Own Words*. New York: PublicAffairs, 2009.

Young, Jeff C. *Political Profiles: Michelle Obama*. Greensboro, North Carolina: Morgan Reynolds, 2009.

## Articles (listed by date of publication)

'Her Plan Went Awry, but Michelle Obama Doesn't Mind.' *Chicago Tribune*, 1 September 2004

'"My Parents Weren't College-educated Folks, so They Didn't Have a Notion of What We Should Want."' *Chicago Sun-Times*, 19 September 2004

'First Lady in Waiting.' *Chicago Magazine*, October 2004

'The Woman Behind Obama.' *Chicago Sun-Times*, 20 January 2007

'Michelle Obama is Hyde Park's Career Mom.' *Hyde Park Herald*, 14 February 2007

'Michelle Obama's Career Timeout.' *Washington Post*, 11 May 2007

'The Natural.' *Vogue*, September 2007

'15th Wedding Anniversary: Obamas Recall First Date, Proposal that "Shut Up" Michelle.' *Chicago Sun-Times*, 3 October 2007

'Michelle Obama Revels in Family Role.' *The Boston Globe*, 28 October 2007

'The Heart and Mind of Michelle Obama.' *O, The Oprah Magazine*, November 2007

'Michelle Obama Solidifies her Role in the Election.' *Wall Street Journal*, 11 February 2008

'Michelle Obama on Love, Family, and Politics.' *CBS Evening News*, 15 February 2008

'Michelle Obama: She's the Closer for her Husband.' *New York Times*, 16 February 2008

'Barack's Rock.' *Newsweek*, 25 February 2008

'Obama's Got Game, says his Brother-in-Law the Coach.' *Providence Journal*, 1 March 2008

'The Other Obama.' *The New Yorker*, 10 March 2008

'Holding Down the Obama Family fort.' *Boston Globe*, 30 March 2008

'She Dresses to Win.' *New York Times*, 9 June 2008

'After Attacks, Michelle Obama Looks for a New Introduction.' *New York Times*, 18 June 2008

'House Rules Help Obama Family Stay Organized.' *People*, 23 July 2008

'Michelle Obama is Vanity Fair's "Best Dressed".' *Los Angeles Times*, 29 July 2008

'The Real Michelle Obama.' *Ebony*, September 2008

'Michelle Obama Tells McCain to End Insults.' *The Times* (UK), 9 October 2008

'A Historic Inauguration Draws Throngs to the Mall.' *Washington Post*, 21 January 2009

'Michelle Obama: The First Lady the World's Been Waiting For.' *Vogue*, March 2009

'Obamas to Plant Vegetable Garden at White House.' *New York Times*, 19 March 2009

'Queen and Michelle Obama – the Story Behind a Touching Moment.' *The Times* (UK), 2 April 2009

'Michelle Obama Finds her Role on the World Stage.' *Time*, 2 April 2009

'A First Lady who Demands Substance.'
*Washington Post*, 25 June 2009

'The World's Most Famous Upper Arms.' *Daily Mail*,
10 September 2009

'Michelle Obama Steps up Policy Role.' *AOL News*,
18 September 2009

'How the Obamas Almost Split up.' *Daily Mail*, 25
September 2009

'In First Lady's Roots, a Complex Path from
Slavery.' *New York Times*, 7 October 2009

# QUOTATIONS FROM SPEECHES OR INTERVIEWS WITH MICHELLE OBAMA AND BARACK OBAMA; OR FROM PUBLISHED TEXTS

**Opening pages**

'We want our children': *Democratic National Convention*, 25 August 2008

'We're all linked': *Washington Post, 2 October 2008*

**Prologue**

'Nothing in my life': *Elizabeth Garrett Anderson School Speech (EGA Speech), April 2009*

**Chapter One**

'I am an example of what is possible when girls, from the very beginning of their lives, are loved and nurtured by the people around them': *EGA Speech, April 2009*

**Chapter Two**

'Deep down inside, I'm still that little girl who
grew up on the South Side of Chicago': *EGA
Speech, April 2009*

**Chapter Three**

'My dad was our rock': *Democratic National
Convention, 2004*

'If my future were determined': *Campaign speech,
18 February 2008*

**Chapter Four**

'I remember being shocked by college students
who drove BMWs': *Telegraph, UK, 26 July
2008*

**Chapter Five**

'By the time she got to Harvard, she had answered
the question. She could be both brilliant and
black': *Michelle's academic advisor [source:
David Brophy, Michelle Obama]*

**Chapter Six**

'Barack Obama was the real deal': *Washington
Post, 11 May 2007*

'His first car had so much rust': *Washington Post*,
5 October 2008

## Chapter Seven
'If what you're doing doesn't bring you joy every
single day, what's the point?' *New York Times*,
16 February 2007

## Chapter Eight
'We know we are blessed': *Campaign speech*,
22 October 2008
'She was the first person I met': *Jose Rico, quoted
in Agence France-Presse, 11 May 2008*

## Chapter Nine
'Every other month since I've had children I've
struggled with the notion of "Am I being a
good parent? Can I stay at home? Should I stay
home? How do I balance it all"?' *Washington
Post*, 11 May 2007
'The Barack Obama I know today': *Democratic
National Convention speech, 25 August 2008*

### Chapter Ten

'She is smart, funny, and thoroughly charming. If I
ever had to run against her for public office,
she would beat me without too much
difficulty': *Barack Obama, quoted in Vogue,
September 2007*

### Chapter Eleven

'There is so much at stake in this election. The
direction of our country hangs in the balance.
We are faced with two clear choices: The world
as it is, and the world as it should be': *quoted
in Michelle Obama, Historical Collector's
Edition, January 2009*

'This is the first sign': *Newsweek*, 25 February
2008

'I'm not here because I'm the wife of a candidate':
*Essence, posted 5 November 2008*

'For the first time': *Campaign speech, 18 February
2008*

'The thing that I've always found':
*television interview with Larry King, 8 October
2008*

### Chapter Twelve

'She's beautifully dressed without too much fuss. She puts on the dress and goes – and it's always a good dress': *Vanity Fair, September 2008*

'Headbands': *Glamour, September 2007*

### Chapter Thirteen

'I come here as a wife who loves my husband and believes he will be an extraordinary president': *Democratic National Convention, 2004*

'We want our children': *Democratic National Convention, 25 August 2008*

'I stand here tonight': *Barack Obama, 25 August 2008*

### Chapter Fourteen

'My first job in all honesty is going to continue to be mom-in-chief': *Ebony magazine, September 2008*

'I'll be mad, but I'll do it': *Marian Robinson; Boston Globe, 30 March 2008*

'It means that we see each other': *People, 21 May 2009*

'Uno is a favourite game': *Rocky Mountain News,*
  *17 July 2008*
'The planting of this garden': *speech to*
  *schoolchildren visiting the White House, quoted*
  *in New York Times, 19 March 2009*
'Dream big, think broadly about your life': *Speech*
  *to graduating seniors at the University of*
  *California-Merced, May 2009*

## Permissions

For all acknowledgements and credits, every effort has been made to trace copyright holders and to credit quotations and sources accurately; but should there be any omissions or corrections needed, the publishers will be happy to correct for subsequent reprints.

## Picture credits

With thanks for the permission to reproduce the photos as follows:

## Cover images

Back cover: Atlas Press / eyevine (Michelle as child); AFP/ Getty Images (speaking at school); Atlas Press / eyevine (graduation)

## Inside colour section 1

i:    Atlas Press / eyevine (Michelle as child)
ii:   Atlas Press / eyevine (graduation), Polaris / eyevine (with Barack);
iii:  Polaris / eyevine (wedding); M. Spencer Green/AP/ Press Association Images (family on sofa)
iv:   New York Times / Redux / eyevine (reaching out); UPI / eyevine (at mic)
v:    UPI / eyevine (swearing in); UPI / eyevine (Inauguration ball); Getty Images (walking with Barack)
vi:   AFP/Getty Images (school visit); Rex Features (with Queen); Getty Images (hosting kids at the White House)
vii:  Haraz N. Ghanbari/AP/Press Association Images (on red carpet); AFP/Getty Images (waving from balcony)

# About the Author

*'Not only is she accomplished, gracious and caring, Michelle Obama has shown the world that a woman can be all those things and still be brilliant. On my list of Phenomenal Women, her name stands out.'*

**Dawne Allette** lives in Baltimore, USA. She was born in Grenada, West Indies, and has lived in Britain and Iran. She is a motivational speaker and a teacher of creative writing. Dawne is also a facilitator of literacy workshops for Baltimore Public Schools and Libraries.

Dawne has written a number of children's picture books that are noted for their inspiration, lyricism and humour. This is her second title for Tamarind Books, following the publication of *Barack Obama: The Making of a President*.

# BARACK OBAMA

## The Making of a President

### by Dawne Allette

*'I, Barack Hussein Obama, do solemnly swear that I will faithfully execute the office of President of the United States . . .'*

On 20 January 2009, history was made as Barack Obama stepped forward to become the President of the USA.

The son of a man from Kenya, he is the first black man ever to hold this post.

The time for change has come.

Follow Barack on his extraordinary journey – growing up as the son of a teenage mother, struggling to find direction as a young man, and ultimately becoming one of the world's most powerful leaders.

**'Hugely readable, dynamic and fascinating'**
*www.readplus.co.uk*

ISBN 978 1 848 53022 5